Ashley Brinton

REACH HIGHER

How You Can Go Beyond Your Personal Limitations, Struggles, and Challenges to Live an Awesome Life and Achieve Your Ultimate Potential

Writing & Publishing Process by PlugAndPlayPublishing.com
Book Cover by Tracey Miller | TraceOfStyle.com
Cover Photography by Natisha Bethers | GuardianOfMemoriesStudios.com
Edited by Lauren Cullumber

ISBN #: 9781099651557

Disclaimer: This book contains opinions, ideas, experiences, and exercises. The purchaser and/or reader of these materials assumes all responsibility for the use of this information. Ashley Brinton and Publisher assume no responsibility and/or liability whatsoever for any purchaser and/or reader of these materials.

To my Grandma, thank you for believing in my ability to read. I can't wait to give you a giant hug when we meet again!

To my handsome husband, Jeffrey, for being my eternity adventure buddy and not allowing me to give up on my dreams!

To both my parents for always cheering me on, supporting me no matter what, and knowing that I could reach higher!

To you – the reader, for allowing me to have an audience to share my message!

Table of Contents

Read This First

Everyone dreams. Little kids dream of rainbows, butterflies, and magical words that come to life. Teenagers dream of love, cars, free food, and the future. Adults dream of success, kids or grandkids, more travel days, retirement, and a bigger house. We all dream.

But some people let challenges, problems, and perceived limitations stop them from achieving their dreams. And some people, when they have failed more times than they care to admit, abandon their dreams and "settle" for what life brings their way. I don't want that to happen to you!

So, unlike other books that talk about dreaming big and achieving success in your life, this book is not going to focus on the dreams and goals. Yes, we'll look at your dreams, goals, and what success means to you. But that will not be our focus. Instead, our focus will be on how you can do anything and achieve anything, no matter the challenges, problems, or limitations – real or perceived – you might feel you have.

I've written this book to help you go beyond your daily normal and reach a little higher. To strive for the success you want. To overcome the obstacles you have. And to be the awesome, unique individual you were destined to be.

The only thing stopping you is you. And my hope is that this book will give you the ideas, actions, and perspective you need to see that even though we all have obstacles in our lives, you can overcome them and have an awesome, excellent, extraordinary life.

How High Can You Reach?

Now, before we get into the nitty gritty, I want to play a game with you. Ready?

Hold your book in your left hand and reach your right hand into the air as high as you can.

Now, reach your hand even higher in the air!

How much higher could you reach? One inch? Two inches? Higher?

Let me ask you a question: is your hand as high as it can go?

You may be saying to yourself, "Yes, Ashley, my hand is as high as it can go!"

Is it? Why aren't you standing up? Or standing on a chair? Or jumping into the air off your chair (be careful!)?

You see, the game wasn't just to reach your hand into the air. The game was meant for you to realize that your mind is the only thing holding you back.

Most people can reach higher the second time I ask. Why? Because we're human, and we rarely reach as high as we can the first time we're asked. Maybe we hold ourselves back because of fear. Maybe we stay within our perceived limits because we're not comfortable putting ourselves out there.

Whatever the reason, what I can tell you from observing thousands of people over the past few years is that most people do what they know they're good at, what feels right, and what they feel is easy. But I know you can do more. I know you can be better!

I have seen my own perceived limitations hold me back. But because of the ideas, actions, and perspectives in this book, I have been able to overcome some of my own personal struggles and transform myself into the woman I am today. So, if you feel lost, alone, and helpless, or if you feel afraid, confused, or even a little "different" – I want you to know that if I can do it, so can you. And this book is here to help you.

How to Get the Most Out of This Book

I've organized this book into 16 easy-to-read chapters that will show you how, even though most of us can't change our limitations, we can overcome our limitations. We just need the right mindset and perspective to see beyond our challenges and see the real truth. In addition, you'll learn tips, tactics, and strategies to help you reach higher and change your life forever.

Inside this book is a plan for you to become the person you know you can become. However, to reach as high as you can, you must mark this book up and make it your own. You must highlight the words that stand out to you, write your own thoughts and feelings in the open margins, and you must act upon the promptings you feel.

I promise that big results will come to you if you use this book to grow yourself as a person. Of course, you should only expect results in your life if, and only if, you follow the plan I have laid out for you. Look, there are no shortcuts to success, so don't just read the words on the page, live the words that are on the page.

And remember that you only get one life. This is your time to shine. This is your time to succeed. This is your time to reach as high as you can!

It's time to get started. By using this book, you'll be able to overcome your personal struggles, reach a little higher, and become the person you know you can become.

Chapter 1
We All Have Challenges (and Dis-Abilities)

In general, the term disability is often used to describe a physical or mental challenge. For example, some of us have obvious disabilities, like autism, paralysis, traumatic brain injury, etc. And some of us have not-so-obvious disabilities, like ADHD, diabetes, anxiety disorder, etc.

I like to refer to disability as dis-ability, because even though you have a specific challenge, in most cases, your dis-ability doesn't hinder you from reaching your true potential. Personally, I struggle with a reading disorder. Now, at first glance, that dis-ability may not seem so bad. However, what if I told you that my dis-ability destroyed one of my childhood dreams?

You see, when I was growing up, I had a dream of being a weather woman, standing in front of a green screen and telling people what style of clothes to wear for the upcoming days: sweaters, shorts, flip-flops, long sleeves.

I wanted that to be my career so badly that I turned our living room into a news room and my family had to come to my "live show" and learn all about the weather each week (that I was clearly making up).

Then, when I was 15 years old, I had the opportunity to go to a live news room set and pretend that I was the weather woman. Honestly, it was a dream come true. I was so excited and so proud that I was nearly bursting out of my skin!

But then I learned something about being a weather woman. Weather women READ their lines! I didn't know that. And, in that moment, my excitement turned to fear...and then into panic...and then into embarrassment as I tried and tried to read my lines.

Imagine for a moment that you have a reading disorder and that you were asked to read out loud in front of an entire group of people. The word "terrifying" doesn't even come close to the angst I felt that day.

I remember crying the entire way home and feeling sorry for myself. But that experience changed my life forever, because I learned on that sad and depressing afternoon that I never wanted my dis-ability to take over my body and my emotions like that ever again!

That's when I made a very important decision. I made the decision to never let my dis-ability stop me from reaching my dreams.

In just a moment, I'm going to ask you to make a decision. However, before I do, I want you to list your challenges, limitations, and "dis-abilities." That way you can see what you're up against and what challenges you'll have to overcome.

Take some time now and jot down any dis-abilities you have in your life:

_____

_____

_____

Your challenges and struggles don't have to be obvious dis-abilities. Maybe you struggle with a reading disorder. Maybe you've been mentally or physically abused in some way. Personally, when I was eight years old, I was told that I was worthless, stupid, and mentally slow. What not-so-obvious dis-abilities have you dealt with in your life? Jot down the words, phrases, thoughts, and heartache you have gone through:

_____

_____

_____

Now, my hope with this exercise is not to downplay the experiences of people who have obvious dis-abilities. The point of this exercise is to make sure you realize that we all have struggles. And more importantly, that you have personal struggles that you're going to have to overcome to reach higher and achieve your full potential.

And now that you know what these personal struggles, challenges, and dis-abilities are…

It's Time for You to Make a Decision

The key to living life with our limitations lies within our decision to not let our dis-abilities stop us from becoming the person we are meant to be.

Every person has a purpose and potential to reach higher, no matter the hurdles they must face. My question to you is this: Are you willing to make the decision to not let your struggles, challenges, and dis-abilities slow you down or stop you?

I hope you answered with a resounding YES!

Listen, I don't know anyone who has a perfect life. Each and every one of us has our own unique challenges, but we also have our own unique potential. The only difference between successful and unsuccessful people is that successful people know their potential and how to focus on their potential at all times.

Before we move into the next chapter, let's play another game right now. Read the next sentence out loud: **I have potential!**

Now say it a little louder: **I HAVE potential!**

Now, as loud as you can, scream: **I HAVE POTENTIAL!**

Your potential doesn't start in the future...it starts now. Make the decision to not let your struggles, challenges, and dis-abilities slow you down or stop you, and I'll see you in the next chapter!

Chapter 2
Not a One-Size-Fits-All

When it comes to success, there is not a one-size-fits all answer. We all define success differently. One person might define success as not having to work more than 40 hours a week, while another person might define success as living at the office but having a million dollars in their bank account.

Both definitions of success are true for each person who defines their success in each way. But, as you can see, both definitions of success are very different. In fact, I'd venture to say that in these two examples, one person's success is the other person's worst nightmare.

So, before you go after your own success, it's important that you define what success means to you. To help you out a little, let me tell you about my definition of success (for me and only me):

Success is:

1. Helping teens and young adults realize their potential in life no matter the obstacles they must overcome

2. Supporting my family with money and time, as in the "fishing story."

Now, you may be wondering what the "fishing story" is all about. A couple years ago, my husband and I read the following story by German author, Heinrich Boll, and it helped us redefine what success meant to us. Here is Boll's story to give you some context:

An American investment banker was at the pier of a small coastal Mexican village when a small boat with just one fisherman docked. Inside the small boat were several large yellowfin tuna. The American complimented the Mexican on the quality of his fish and asked how long it took to catch them.

The Mexican replied, "Only a little while." The American then asked why didn't he stay out longer and catch more fish. The Mexican said he had enough to support his family's immediate needs. The American then asked, "But what do you do with the rest of your time?"

The Mexican fisherman said, "I sleep late, fish a little, play with my children, take siestas with my wife, Maria, stroll into the village each evening, where I sip wine and play guitar with my amigos. I have a full and busy life." The American scoffed, "I am a Harvard MBA and could help you. You should spend more time fishing and with the proceeds, buy a bigger boat. With the proceeds from the bigger boat, you could buy several boats, eventually you would have a fleet of fishing boats. Instead of selling your catch to a middleman, you would sell directly to the processor, eventually opening your own cannery. You would control the product, processing, and distribution. You would need to leave this small coastal fishing village and move to Mexico City, then LA and eventually New York City, where you will run your expanding enterprise."

The Mexican fisherman asked, "But, how long will this all take?"

To which the American replied, "15 – 20 years."

"But what then?" Asked the Mexican.

The American laughed and said, "That's the best part. When the time is right you would announce an IPO and sell your company stock to the public and become very rich, you would make millions!"

"Millions – then what?"

The American said, "Then you would retire. Move to a small coastal fishing village where you would sleep late, fish a little, play with your kids, take siestas with your wife, stroll to the village in the evenings where you could sip wine and play your guitar with your amigos."

The Mexican fisherman replied, "Isn't that what I am already doing?"

Like I said, you must have your own definition of success. Boll's story touched us so deeply that my husband and I have redefined what success means to us.

When you read what success means to me, do you have to understand my definition? No! My definition of success is *my own* definition of success. Outside this book, no one else has to know what my definition of success means. I'm the only person who must know what it means.

The same is true for you. Only you can decide and define what success means to you.

Defining Your Success

What does success look like to you? Below are five categories that will help you define your success:

- Money
- Relationships
- Dis-Ability
- Career
- Free Time

In order to identify your ultimate success, you need to identify success in each of those five categories. I will help you jump start your thought process in each category. Let's start with…

Success Category #1: Money

When it comes to this success category, there are two types of people in the world: those who define their success with having a specific amount of money, and those who define their success with what money can provide.

For example, some people define their success by making $50,000 a year. Others define their success by making $100,000 a year or by making $1 Million a year. The specific amount will vary per person. The point here is, if your definition of success is about having a specific salary every year, it's important that you choose a specific dollar figure that you feel is important to you.

I have a friend who has built her life and success around the idea of making a specific dollar amount. Her definition of success includes making $100,000+ a year. For her, the amount of money she takes home and the amount of money she has in the bank define how successful she is. To be clear, there is nothing wrong with defining your success based on the money you want to make.

If you're this type of person, write down how much money you want to make each year: $_____

On the flip side, your definition of success may not include a specific dollar amount. Instead, you may define success based on what money can provide for you and your family. For instance, you may define success as having the ability to pay bills without having debt; or you may define success as having the money to live in an elaborate mansion and drive a fancy car.

Personally, I don't identify my ultimate success with how much money I make. Rather, I define my success based on what I can do with money. Here's a short list of what we're looking to achieve with the money we make (at the time of this writing):

- Buy our dream house
- Travel a minimum of one family vacation and one couple vacation every year
- Save more money for our kids' college fund and our retirement fund
- Have money for our kids to play sports and be involved in extracurricular activities

Are you the type of person who defines your success based on what money can provide for you and your family? If so, take some time now and jot down some ideas of what you will do with the money you earn:

_____

_____

_____

Success Category #2: Relationships

Sometimes our relationships give us the love and support we need. Other times, our relationships drain our energy and create drama in our life. For your success (and your sanity), it's important to define what you feel each relationship should look like and feel like.

For example, here are three of my relationships and how I define what they should look and feel like to be successful:

- Parents: I want my relationship with my parents to feel like a parent-child relationship where I can safely share moments and experiences and get the guidance I need. In addition, I want us to be able to talk to each other like adults where we discuss real life topics and have a special, respective friendship.

- Spouse: I want my relationship with my spouse to feel like a merged or combined force. Meaning, I want us to be a unified team and always support one another. In addition, I want us to always build each other up and place each other's needs before our own. We are building our dreams together, and we're making our personal dreams a "together dream" - and we won't stop until we achieve our success.

- Friends: I want my relationships with each of my friends to share a similar interest, hobby, or passion. In addition, I want us to always build each other up and positively support each other in the decisions we make.

Now it's your turn. Take a moment and write down how you want each relationship in your life to look and feel like:

_____

_____

_____

Now that you know what you're looking for from each relationship, it's time to determine if your current relationships really do look and feel like you want them to.

I'm blessed because the relationship I have with my spouse is exactly how I described and exactly how I always wanted it to be. However, not all of my relationships have fit my definition of success.

For example, when I was in high school, I had a "friend" named Kathy (not her real name) who was downright evil. Kathy would always say hurtful things to me and others. She would always put me down. And she would always tell me things I should hate about myself. Not much of a friend, right?

As you can see, my relationship with Kathy was not a healthy friendship. Sadly, I didn't realize how toxic our relationship was until I finally noticed that I was starting to act like her. I was being mean to my parents, mean to my family, and mean my other friends. That's when my mom intervened (thank goodness!) and helped me see what was going on.

With some much-needed guidance, I had to re-evaluate my "friendship" with Kathy. The decision I ultimately came to was to cut her out of my life. Trust me when I say this, my decision was not an easy one!

But it was the right decision, because my relationship with Kathy drained my energy, changed my mood and attitude, and was preventing me from becoming the person I was meant to be.

Now, was she doing all this on purpose? Probably not. But, nevertheless, my decision to cut ties was one of the best decisions of my life.

You may have a relationship in your life that doesn't fit your definition of success. If that's the case, then I suggest seeking professional counsel to help you make the right, mature decision. Will you have to cut someone out of your life? Maybe. Maybe not. That's for you to decide with the help of your parents, counselor, or therapist.

My point here is to evaluate your relationships and make sure they fit with your definition of success. Associating with the right people is a key part of your ultimate success.

Take some time and think about the relationships you have in your life. What do you feel they should look like, and what do they actually look like? If the reality of a relationship isn't congruent with your definition of success, then think about how you can make the relationship better, and what steps you need to take to make that happen:

Success Category #3: Dis-Ability

To have the success we desire, we must factor in our personal dis-ability. After all, your dis-ability is a part of who you are, and, therefore, it follows you around everywhere you go. Remember though, success is something you choose, create, and label for yourself. So, when you think about your success in life, where does your dis-ability fit in?

Personally, my dis-ability was a stepping stone in my life to get me to where I am. For starters, my dis-ability taught me how to be a more understanding person. Because I have a reading dis-ability, and I must read with a dictionary by my side (I use my cellphone and google translate), I know what it is like to feel stupid or left out. So, when I see others that also look like they are struggling with a seemingly easy task, I am never quick to judge, because I too know what it is like to look like an outcast. If it wasn't for my dis-ability, I may not have the compassion for others that I do now. My dis-ability taught me that valuable lesson and many other life lessons. And my dis-ability has help shape me into the person I am today.

But I'm not the only person to incorporate my dis-ability into my success. Let's take a look at some famous figures through history who have done the same:

1. Abraham Lincoln is said to be one of the greatest Presidents to ever live. But did you know that Lincoln faced many struggles, challenges, and defeats in his life? Abraham Lincoln lost eight elections. He suffered a nervous breakdown. And he failed miserably in business. However, he never quit, and he later became the 16th President of the United States.

2. Albert Einstein could not speak until he was four years old, and he could not read until he was nine years old. In addition, he had teachers that described him as "mentally slow." However, despite his setbacks and dis-abilities, Einstein became arguably the greatest scientist of all time.

3. Helen Keller was born in the United States in 1880 with an illness that left her both blind and deaf before she was two years old. However, Helen's roadblocks and dis-abilities did not stop her from reaching higher. Among many accomplishments in her life, Helen Keller holds the title of first deaf-blind person to earn a Bachelor of Arts.

Did these famous people let their dis-abilities slow them down? No. They persisted no matter what they faced. In fact, you can even say that their dis-abilities came to define their success. Don't believe me? Then why are we still talking about these amazing people decades and even a full century after their deaths?

You see, the only real roadblock in our life is our lack of seeing our success beyond our dis-ability. So, let me ask you this: how will your dis-ability be a stepping stone in your journey? In the space below, write about how your dis-ability will not stop you from reaching higher and how your disability will define your success:

_____

_____

_____

"Disability need not be an obstacle to success."
– Stephen Hawking

Success Category #4: Career

No matter what career path you choose, it's important to consider how your career choice will fit into the overall success you desire for your life. After all, the average American spends between 1800 – 2000 hours (or more) at work every single year. Who would want to spend that time working in a career that didn't support their bigger goals and dreams?

So, what are some goals you'd like to achieve with your career? Is the title you hold important to you? Do you need an office with a view? Does the location you live in for work matter to you? Do you want to work longer hours but be your own boss? Do you want to work shorter hours but work for someone else? Do you want your career to involve travel? Does the focus of your career matter to you?

I know. There are a lot of variables to think about. Take a moment now and jot down some ideas:

_____

_____

_____

Now that you have some ideas of what you'd like to accomplish with your career, let me give you two of my career goals. My hope is that my examples inspire you to think of new ideas for your own career path. However, even after reading my goals, it's a great idea to ask other people you know what they love and hate about their careers. This "research" may give you some insight into what a successful career could look like for you.

Since my dis-ability shaped my entire career, I wanted a career that focused on the topic of helping others overcome their dis-abilities. Hence you reading this book and why I'm a professional speaker who travels the world teaching others that they, too, can live with hardships that come their way.

Helping others reach their dreams is a career that feels right to me and fits into the way I see success in my life.

Another main goal I have in my career is freedom. I love being my own boss. I love working when I want and not answering to anyone. That's not to say I don't work hard or that I don't work long hours. I do. I just have more flexibility and freedom than I would have if I worked for someone else. Trust me. I know. I worked for someone else for four years. I loved my job, but I knew working for myself was my ultimate goal to achieve the career success I wanted. My husband, on the other hand, couldn't be his own boss, because I don't think he would ever get anything done. Not because he is lazy – he's an extremely hard worker – but because he needs the structure a job provides.

Now, your goals don't have to resonate with my goals. Again, my purpose in telling you some of my career goals was to inspire you with new ideas that you may not have thought about. Did it work? Did you think of new career ideas that you'd like to incorporate into your definition of success? If so, take a moment and add to your list above.

Success Category #5: Free Time

A conversation about success wouldn't be complete without us talking about free time. Why? Because life isn't just about working. Life is about living. What people do in their free time is what excites them and what makes life worth the hard work and struggles they face.

So, what do you like to do in your free time? What hobbies do you have? What passions do you enjoy? Take some time now and jot down the activities you enjoy most and want to incorporate into your definition of success:

_____

_____

_____

How you spend your free time will also determine how much energy you have to take care of your family, spend time with your friends, and enjoy your career. You see, free time is like charging a cellphone. No matter what brand of cellphone you have, you must recharge it at some point.

Some people charge their cellphone every night. Some people go, go, go, until their phone is close to losing battery power before they recharge it. Some people charge them on a plane, in their car, or on a train. The point is this, no matter where or when you recharge your cellphone, you must recharge it at some point – if you want to use it again.

The same is true for people. To live, love, and enjoy life, we must recharge our batteries, too.

However, since we all recharge differently, it's important to figure out how you recharge best. For example, some people recharge by being around other people, while some people prefer being alone. That's me and my husband to a "T." I like to journal or read a book in a public place, like a library or restaurant, while my husband likes to read a book without anyone around.

Recharging your batteries is essential to your emotional, physical, and mental well-being. Take some time now and think about how you like to recharge your batteries. Write your answers in the lines provided:

_____

_____

_____

Success Motto

Now that you have fleshed out what success looks like to you using the above five categories, it is time to simplify your definition of success and write your success motto!

Your success motto can be as long or as short as you would like it to be. However, I would encourage you to make your success motto easy to remember and something you can repeat without any thought. After all, we want this motto to be the driving force behind your decisions moving forward.

Take a moment now, and jot down your new success motto. Don't worry. You can change your mind and tweak your motto later after you gain more clarity on what you want your life to look like. For now, write down an easy-to-remember phrase or motto of what success is to you:

_____

_____

_____

If you need some additional help, here is my success motto again:

Success is helping teens and young adults realize their potential in life no matter the obstacles they must overcome while supporting my family with money and time, like the "fishing story."

Feel free to use my success motto as a "model" – do not steal my motto, but use it to inspire your own success motto.

Once you have your success motto, write it down and hang it up by your bed, in your locker, and/or in a notebook. You want to make sure you see it a lot during your day. That way, your motto is always top of mind and a focal point of your thoughts.

Your Definition of Success Can and Will Change

Before we end this chapter, I want to make something clear. Your definition of success can and will change as you evolve into the person you are meant to be. So, don't feel like you're locked into your success motto. You can change your definition of success as you achieve new successes, as well as when you make new distinctions about what you want for your life.

To help paint a clearer picture, let me explain what success used to look like for me, and what success looks like now. A few years ago, success was doing well in school and jump-starting my speaking career path. Then, my definition of success changed when I was hired by my dream company at the age of 18. Then, at the age of 22, my definition of success changed again when I decided I was ready to live out my dream of becoming a keynote speaker for high schools, colleges, and youth/young adult organizations all over the country, while owning my own business.

As you can see, my definition of success has changed a few times over the years. And it will continue to change as I get older and get better.

And yours will too. But in order to reach higher than you ever have before, in order to jumpstart your life today, right now, you need to understand what that success is to you!

So, take the time to do the above exercises and write out your success motto. Your personal success motto will remind you of who you are, what you stand for, and where you are headed.

"
Success doesn't
live in one part of
your life and
become exempt
in another.

— Steve Harvey

Chapter 3
The S.M.A.R.T. Path

It takes time, energy, and a lot of thought to figure out what you want for your future. Congratulations, you just did a great job! You should be proud!

Now it is time to dive even deeper by making a plan and creating a path for reaching your success vision. In this chapter, we're going to do that by focusing on creating S.M.A.R.T. goals for each of your success categories.

What Does S.M.A.R.T. Stand For?

S.M.A.R.T. is an acronym that stands for:

Specific: Your goals must be simply written and clearly defined.

Measurable: Your goals must be measurable and quantifiable. Meaning, you should be able to determine when you reach a specific goal.

<u>A</u>chievable: Your goals must be achievable. In other words, you must possess the appropriate knowledge, skills, and abilities needed to achieve the goal. If you don't possess the appropriate knowledge, skills, and abilities, you must make sure you have access to resources that will help you learn and grow in the areas you lack, so you can accomplish the goal down the line.

<u>R</u>elevant: Your goals must be relevant to who you are, what you stand for, and what you want for your future.

<u>T</u>ime-bound: Your goals must have deadlines attached to them. Deadlines not only keep you on task, deadlines also help create a sense of urgency and pressure that help you achieve your goals.

To help you see this more clearly, let me give you an example of a S.M.A.R.T. goal. Let's say your success vision for your Money category is making $100,000 per year by age 25. That's a great goal! However, since that achievement will not just land in your lap as you sit on the couch, we must create a S.M.A.R.T. goal to help you achieve your vision.

An example may look like this: I'm going to send out five applications by August 1st to be an intern at jobs that pay $100,000 per year once hired full-time.

Is that goal specific? Yes. You're going to send out five intern applications to jobs that pay the salary you desire.

Is that goal measurable? Yes. You're going to send out five applications by August 1st.

Is that goal achievable? Yes. If you possess the knowledge, skills, and abilities to do the job.

Is that goal relevant? Yes. Since you want to make $100,000 per year, applying to jobs that pay $100,000 per year is relevant.

Is that goal time-bound? Yes. You're going to send out the applications by August 1st.

Now, this goal is just an example. Your S.M.A.R.T. goal may be completely different. The point is that if you make your goals S.M.A.R.T. goals, you'll be more likely to reach your goals because your S.M.A.R.T. goals help you lay out a path to achieve what you desire.

Create Your Own S.M.A.R.T. Goals

Now, it's your turn to create S.M.A.R.T. goals for each of the five success categories we looked at in Chapter 2. Use the lines below to create your own S.M.A.R.T. goals:

Money goal(s):

_____

_____

_____

Relationships goal(s):

_____

_____

_____

Dis-Ability goal(s):

_____

_____

_____

Career goal(s):

_____

_____

_____

Free Time goal(s):

_____

_____

_____

Are your S.M.A.R.T. goals specific, measurable, achievable, relevant, and time-bound? If so, then move on. If not, please try rewriting your goals until you make each goal a S.M.A.R.T. goal.

Now that you have created S.M.A.R.T. goals in each of the five categories, you have the beginnings of a "smart path" to help you achieve the future you desire. Of course, you may have to create more S.M.A.R.T. goals along the way or adjust the ones you fail at accomplishing.

For now, you have a plan to start your journey. Keep these goals top of mind throughout the rest of this book as we explore tips, tactics, and much more to help you achieve your goals and reach your ultimate potential.

Chapter 4
Master Your Mindset

So far, you've decided to not let any struggle, roadblock, or "dis-ability" stop you from reaching higher in your life. In addition, you've also determined what success looks like to you, created your Success Motto, and created some S.M.A.R.T. goals to help you achieve your vision of success.

In this chapter, we're going to look at the mindset you'll need to reach higher and achieve the success you want, no matter what obstacles are put in your way. When it comes to mindset, there are two main concepts we'll cover here:

1. Overcoming > Change

2. Weakness + Strength

Overcoming > Change

When I was in math class, I struggled with all the rules because they made no sense to me. For some reason, "X" was always missing, and "Y" could never be found! However, the one thing I loved about math class was the awesome games you could play to figure out certain answers.

For example, did you know that you can figure out the multiples of nine with your fingers? It's true! Here's how:

1. Place your hands in front of you, palms facing you, as if you were going to use your fingers to count to ten.

2. Think of a number (1-10) that you want to multiply nine by. Let's choose the number "4".

3. Count "4" fingers from the left and put down your 4th finger (in this case, your ring finger on your left hand).

4. Count the fingers to the left of the 4th finger, and then count the fingers to the right of the 4th finger. You should have counted three fingers on your left side and six fingers on the right side. That's your answer: 3 and 6 – or 36. So, by using this method, you can easily figure out the multiples of 9. In this case, 9 x 4 = 36.

Isn't that cool?! Try calculating any of the first ten multiples of nine. Your fingers never lie. I love that game. It made it easy and fun to learn.

Do you know another math game I loved? (Stay with me here, I have a point.) It's the "greater than and less than" game. Have you ever played it?

When I was younger, the terms "greater than" and "less than" never made sense to me. So, my mom taught me the "greater than and less than" game, where you call the symbols indicating greater than and less than "alligator mouth" symbols. She said the alligator always wants to eat the bigger side. So, if we take the numbers 5 and 12, which number does the alligator want to eat? The 12, right? So, your alligator mouth would face the 12 and the equation would look like this: $5 < 12$.

So, what does the "greater than and less than" game have to do with overcoming obstacles in your life?

Overcoming is greater than change (overcoming > change). Meaning, it's more important to focus on overcoming your obstacles, your struggles, your dis-abilities, than it is to try and change them.

If you were born blind, you can't change that. If you are in a wheelchair, you can't change that. So, instead of trying to change those facts, we want to focus our energy and attention on overcoming those obstacles.

So, if you're in a wheelchair, what can you do to overcome your situation? Do some research and find a role model who's overcome a challenge like yours. The late Stephen Hawking jumps to my mind. Just because he was in a wheelchair, he overcame his "dis-ability" to write books, become a professor, and even gain celebrity status. Stephen Hawking is the perfect example of "nothing is out of your reach if you have the mindset to reach higher!"

Personally, my reading dis-ability made it hard for me to focus in school. After numerous tests, my doctors recommended my parents put me on medication to help me focus. In other words, they tried to "change" my dis-ability.

My mom told me that I was on the medicine for one week, and by the seventh day, she was crying and asking for her little girl back. You see, the medication did make me more focused. But it also made me mean, more annoyed by simple tasks, and not the happy, enthusiastic person that I was and am today.

By day eight my parents took me off the medicine, and according to my mom, "the difference was night and day, and I had my little girl back."

Now, don't get me wrong. The doctors and my parents meant well. And, in some cases, medication may be the right answer for some people. I'm certainly not a doctor, and I'm in no way giving medical advice.

However, for me, changing my dis-ability with medicine wasn't the answer. Sure, it solved one problem with my dis-ability, but it also caused more problems than I had before. And that is what change often does.

More often than not, change adds more problems than it solves. That's why we want to focus on overcoming our obstacles and dis-abilities, because overcoming is greater (i.e. more important) than change.

Master the Mindset of Overcoming

So, how do you develop the mindset of overcoming your obstacles and dis-abilities? Here are four tips to help you master the mindset of overcoming.

Tip #1: Keep a Positive Attitude

Keeping a positive attitude helps you cope more easily, and it brings optimism into your life. In a world that can be negative and pessimistic, your attitude and optimism go a long way in keeping you focused on overcoming what's in front of you versus trying to change what's in front of you.

Now, like I said, we live in a negative and pessimistic world, so keeping a positive attitude may be difficult some days. The trick I use to stay positive is to find a way to laugh at the situation. Even if the situation is not funny, I make myself laugh now.

Listen, nine times out of ten, you'll laugh at a situation years after it happens. Why wait? When something negative happens, envision yourself five years from now laughing at the situation…and start to laugh now.

Give this little trick a shot and see if it boosts your mood and attitude. It does for me (almost) every time.

Tip #2: Focus on Your End Result

Don't exchange your end result for a simple pleasure now. In other words, if you're trying to lose weight, you don't want to exchange losing ten pounds (your end result) for a chocolate chip cookie (simple pleasure) today. If you do, then you'll never hit your end goal.

The best way to focus on your end result is to see your goal or your vision for the future on a daily basis. One way to do that is to create a vision board. Here's how my family created a vision board for our dreams and goals:

First, we bought a poster board. Then, we googled pictures that matched our success goals, printed the pictures and glued them to the poster board (our vision board). Next, we wrote a few words by each picture, so we could remember what that picture represented. And finally, we hung our new vision board up in our living room, so we could see our dreams and goals (the end result we want) every day.

Some people create vision boards for their whole life. Others, like me, create a new vision board each year with goals for just that year. The choice is up to you. I encourage you to at least create a vision board for your success goals, so you can focus on the end results you want in your life.

Tip #3: Discover Tools and Resources

In today's technology-driven world, there are tools and resources to help you overcome almost any challenge in life. For example, even though I have a reading dis-ability, I love to read!

Growing up, reading was a struggle and a challenge. But, today, reading is one of my favorite pastimes. Why? Because of the tools and resources I now have at my disposal.

Google has become one of my best friends. When I read, I make sure Google is close by, so I can type a word in and hear how the word sounds, see the definition, and even see how the word is used in other sentences. Yes, reading takes me more time than most. But Google, as a tool, is one way I am able to enjoy the pleasure of reading.

Another tool I utilize is Google Translate. I comprehend better when things are read out loud to me. So, when I receive an email, I have my personal assistant, Google Translate, read me the email. She's awesome!

Do you have tools and resources that you use to help you with your challenges and dis-abilities? Take a moment and jot them down here:

_____

_____

_____

What other tools and resources are at your disposal that you may not know about? Take some time now and research some tools and resources that you may find beneficial. If you need help, my girl, Google, can help you.

When you find the tools and resources that can help you, jot them down here:

_____

_____

_____

Tip #4: You Have to Be ALL-IN

In the game of poker, if someone says they are "all-in," it means that they are putting the last of their chips (money) into the pot. The same is true in life. There's no time to tiptoe around what you want. In order to achieve what you want to and overcome your dis-ability, you have to be ALL-IN.

For example, when I worked at Plato's Closet, a clothing store, we had a rule that was easy to understand but a challenge to complete. For every five hours you worked, you had to give out three customer hold bins. If you completed this task, you received the employee discount for the whole next month. If you did not complete this task, you did not get the employee discount.

Well, there was no way I was working at a clothing store and not getting the employee discount. That wasn't an option. No matter what I had to do, I was ALL-IN.

So, what happened? I never missed a month at getting my employee discount. Why? Because I was all-in. Like I said, missing the opportunity to save money on clothes wasn't even an option. I knew I wanted clothes, and I knew that I couldn't justify paying full price when I knew how to earn the employee discount. So, I went all-in and hit that goal every month.

Yes, being all-in takes hard work, passion, and determination. But, in order to truly have the mindset to overcome your dis-ability, being all-in is a must.

Weakness + Strength = AWESOMENESS

As you can see, we are back to math. But this time, we're looking at a simple addition equation – **Weakness + Strength = Awesomeness** – where your weakness equals your dis-ability and your strength equals your dis-ability.

Wait, what? How can both variables equal the same thing? The short answer is, they don't equal one another. However, they do relate to one another. Let's play a quick game to understand the equation and how both variables parallel each other.

On page 46, you will see a table. One side contains weaknesses and the other side contains strengths that correlate with each weakness. For example, the first weakness is, "It's hard for me to sit still," and the first strength is, "This makes me really fun at dance parties."

Do you see how the perceived weakness relates to the strength? Take a look at the rest of the examples in the table.

Weakness	Strength
It's hard for me to sit still	This makes me really fun at dance parties
I struggle to tell people no	I'm great at helping people when it is short notice
I struggle reading basic English	I am more understanding of where others are coming from
I can't focus on one task for too long	I learn how to adapt and go with the flow

As you can see, the perceived weakness and related strength are not the same. But they do relate to each other and have a direct correlation with each other.

In fact, I'd argue that if it was not for your weakness(es) you would not have the related strength(s).

This is important because if you're going to succeed in spite of your weaknesses and dis-abilities, you must master the mindset of **Weakness + Strength = Awesomeness**. Meaning, your awesomeness comes from both your weaknesses AND your strengths.

Master the Mindset of Weaknesses

So, how do you master the mindset of weaknesses? Here are three tips to help you see that **Weakness + Strength = Awesomeness**.

Tip #1: Weaknesses Correlate to Strengths

As you saw in the table on page 46, there is a strength for every weakness. What I'd like you to do now is use the table below and write down your weaknesses and each weakness' corresponding strength.

Weakness	Strength

Sometimes, admitting to ourselves or others that we struggle with something can bring us down. However, it's important to realize that without your dis-ability, you would not have the correlating strengths you have today.

Our strengths come from our weaknesses. They're blessings in disguise.

Tip #2: Focus Makes Perfect

We have all heard the saying: practice makes perfect. But from here on out, I want to adapt that saying to: focus makes perfect. Why? Because focus is at the heart of your success and your ability to reach higher.

When we focus on a task or on our goals, we are able to perform at our best. When we are not focused on a task or on our goals, we cannot and do not perform at our best. Focus is extremely important, and when we don't stay focused on our goals, the only person we cheat is ourselves.

So, the question now becomes, "How do I stay focused on my goals, so I can see my goals and dreams come to fruition?" Luckily, we have already talked about two ways to stay focused each and every day:

- Create your personal success motto and place your motto in three places you can see every day

- Create a vision board and place it in a place you can see every day

Another way to stay focused on your tasks and goals is to have a system for tracking your progress on a daily basis. For example, some people use their smartphone to track their goals. Others use a spreadsheet on their computer. Personally, I am a paper type of girl, so I journal and mark up my vision board. The method matters less than the action. Keep track and focus on your goals with whatever method works best for you.

The only way you can master the mindset of your weaknesses is to know where you stand with your weaknesses. By keeping track of your progress, you will know how far you've come and how far you have left to go.

Plus, when you track your progress, if something goes wrong or you're going off course, you can see the mistake or error and fix things before time is wasted or it becomes too late to make a change.

Remember, focus makes perfect. When we focus on keeping ourselves strong in everything we do, we will find more success than we originally imagined.

Tip #3: Know Your WHY NOT!

I'll tell you right now, if you know your WHY (i.e. why you do what you do), then you will be successful. Those who know why they do what they do are the ones who reach higher and achieve new heights every day.

Knowing your why is motivational. Knowing your why is inspirational. And knowing why will help remind you that sometimes the nonsense you have to go through in life is worth every struggle, every challenge, and every dis-ability or weakness you may have.

In addition to knowing your why, it's just as important to know your WHY NOT. As in, "why not go for it!"

It's a liberating feeling when you can say, "why not, I'm going for it" or "screw it, I'm going for it" or "YOLO, I'm going for it."

The moment I decided to live my WHY NOT was the moment I left my comfort zone to live the life of my dreams. I was working a good paying, full time job with health benefits, and I was not only supporting my family's current needs but also our current wants.

But I knew that I was not living my success motto. So, I quit my day job, went to work for myself, and have found that success was just past my comfort zone.

Now, don't take that the wrong way. You need to think these things through and make mature decisions for your family and for your life. But when you change the conversation in your mind from "I can't do that" to "why not, I'm going for it," your world will completely change, and your goals and dreams will be one step closer.

"You will never make it. You're not smart enough. Your dream is just a fun idea, not a real, achievable goal. Stop wasting your time.

It's not worth the time because you will never see results..." Those are just some of the negative comments I heard growing up. But, deep down, I always knew that if I didn't try, I would always wonder "what if."

Stop playing the "what if" game! Instead, play the "why not" game and go for it!

Do the things that you have always wanted to do but have never done without worrying about the judgement of others. Stand up and say that you can and will reach higher than you have ever reached before.

Living your WHY NOT is when you do what you were meant to do – what you know in your heart and in your gut to be true for you.

Look, your weaknesses and dis-abilities will stop you if you let them. But, if you master your mindset, let your weaknesses become your strengths, focus on your goals and dreams, and change the conversation in your mind from "what if" to "why not," then you will become the awesome person you were meant to be.

Chapter 5

Become Fluent in Your Success Language

L anguage is interesting because even though most people in America speak English, not all of us use the same
words to describe what we're talking about. Don't believe
me? Let's play another game, so I can show you. Below,
you'll find a commonly used item in America. Circle which
word/phrase you use to describe this item:

1. Bubbler

2. Water Cooler

3. Drinking Fountain

4. Water Fountain

Which word/phrase do you use? I say drinking fountain. In
fact, most people in the western states say drinking fountain.
However, water fountain is commonly used in the central

states and bubbler is commonly used in parts of Wisconsin, Massachusetts, and Rhode Island.

As you can see, even though we all speak the same language, there are nuances used across the country. That's why the words you use matter. The right words will help you reach higher. The wrong words will keep you from reaching your true potential.

So, what are the right words? The right words make up your success language and are determined by your goals and the type of success you want for your future. To reach higher and achieve the success you envision, it's imperative that you become fluent in your own success language.

But how? How do you become fluent in your own success language? Here are two steps to help you become fluent in your own success language:

Step #1: Identify Others Who Speak Your Success Language

Do you have a friend who you get along with really well? In most cases it's because you both speak the same language and have the same interests. Romantic relationships are similar in nature. When you speak the same language and have the same interests as your boyfriend or girlfriend, you both "click" and get along with each other. It's easy. Like breathing.

The same is true for people who speak your success language. When you find your "tribe," and everyone speaks the same success language, you can grow your success "vocabulary" and reach higher together.

Let me give you a personal example. When I was 18, I discovered that my parents and my friends spoke a different success language than I did. It's not that my parents and my friends are bad people. They are awesome, and I love them all! But we define success differently, and we have different directions we want to go in life. Therefore, we speak a little differently. So, in order for me to reach higher, I needed to identify with someone that spoke my language. Someone that was on the same path as me. That's when I discovered that keynote speakers who spoke to student-aged audiences spoke my success language. When I heard these speakers from the stage, it was like music to my ears. They had the same vision I did, and they used the same words I did.

So, who speaks your success language? Do business men or women speak your language? Do stay-at-home parents speak your language? Do professional athletes speak your language? Who speaks your success language?

Use the lines below and write down who speaks your language:

_____

_____

_____

Step #2: Immerse Yourself in the Culture

In 2012, my husband Jeff moved to Mexico for a church mission. Before moving, Jeff took two months of Spanish classes. However, he tells people that while the classes were good, it wasn't until he was immersed in the culture that the real learning began.

In fact, within eight months of living in Mexico, Jeff was fluent in Spanish. And when asked by locals how long he had been speaking the language, they were always shocked by his answer.

Now, let's compare Jeff's experience to my sister Gabie. Gabie has taken high school Spanish classes for the past three years. But all she can do is count to 50, ask you where the bathroom is, and say a few pickup lines. Don't get me wrong. Gabie is a 4.0 student with more than a few scholarships at her fingertips. She's wicked smart.

But the difference between Jeff's experience and Gabie's experience is night and day.

Gabie likes Spanish, but speaking the language isn't a necessity. Meaning, if she isn't fluent in Spanish she still survives and lives life as usual. Jeff, on the other hand, couldn't afford that luxury. If Jeff did not learn Spanish, and learn it fast, he would not have been able to live life in Mexico.

Imagine not being able to order food, find a bathroom, or make a friend. If Jeff didn't learn the language, then he would have been completely lost and he would not have been able to accomplish what he set out to do.

The same is true for you and learning your success language. To become fluent in your success language, you must immerse yourself in the culture!

Now, most of us can't be like Jeff and move to a whole new country for two years to learn and live our language of success. But you can immerse yourself in different ways.

For example, I started by reading books and watching YouTube videos of keynote speakers. Then, I started attending conferences where keynote speakers gathered. As my success language vocabulary grew, I even emailed keynote speakers that I had never met before to see if they would take a call with me and tell me how they got started.

So, how will you immerse yourself into the culture of your language? Take a moment and jot down some ideas:

_____

_____

_____

Because each of us has a different vision of success, each of us will have a different language of success. I challenge you to start today and become fluent in your success language.

Start by identifying those who speak your language, and then immerse yourself in the culture. Using these steps will help you pick up on the language faster and learn valuable lessons you can't learn otherwise.

Chapter 6
Words Can Heal
or They Can Hurt

The words you speak to yourself are powerful and can affect your attitude. For example, say this out loud: "I'm SO tired." Say it again, "I'm soooooo tired!" Now, how do you feel? I play this game with audiences all the time, and do you know how most people feel when they say this out loud? Tired. Crazy, isn't it?

Now, go ahead and say out loud, "I feel GREAT!" Say it again, but this time like Tony the Tiger: "I feel grrrrreat!" Now, how do you feel? I bet you feel better than you did a moment ago. To reach higher, you must pick the words you say to yourself carefully. After all, they affect how you feel, how you think, and how you act.

But the words you use don't stop with you. The words you speak to others are influential too. For example, have you ever been told something that really upset you, or something that made you over the moon excited? I'm betting you answered YES. If so, then you know how powerful words are.

Words can heal or they can hurt. Words can build someone up or they can tear someone down. Words can make someone's day bright and sunny or dark and rainy. Words can shift someone's mood from love to hate or from pride to disappointment in a heartbeat. And words can stick with you for years...even decades.

For instance, when I was a junior in high school and a member of Family, Career, and Community Leaders of America (FCCLA), I was on the fence about running to be one of ten National Officers for FCCLA (this is a big deal in that world). I was nervous and scared, but the words in my head that pushed me to run for the position came from Utah FCCLA's State Family and Consumer Science Specialist a few years earlier.

She said, "Ashley, you are Utah FCCLA's *secret weapon*." That sentence changed my life, and those words have stuck with me ever since. Her words were the motivation I needed to run for National Office.

Spoiler alert: I was elected that year, and although I have many to thank, that sentence was the push I needed.

Order Matters

Believe it or not, the way we word a sentence can affect the entire meaning, and can affect the outcome of a situation. I'll show you. Let's play a game. In this game, we will be moving the position of the same word to create different sentences with different meanings.

The word we are going to move is: "only."

The sentence we are going to use is: "He told his girlfriend that he loved her."

Here are three version of the above sentence:

- He told his *only* girlfriend that he loved her

- He told his girlfriend that *only* he loved her.

- He told his girlfriend that he loved *only* her.

Here is what each sentence means to me:

"He told his *only* girlfriend that he loved her." To me, this sentence is cute. He is telling the only girl he has that he loves her. What does this sentence mean to you?

"He told his girlfriend that *only* he loved her." To me, this sentence is harsh. He is telling his girlfriend that no one else loves her. Only he loves her. What does this sentence mean to you?

"He told his girlfriend that he loved *only* her." To me, this sentence is saying he might be dating around, but he is telling *this* girl, his girlfriend, that he loves only her. What does this sentence mean to you?

Do you see how the order of the words matters? Remember that we control what comes out of our mouths. We control how we say something. Let's put conscious effort into choosing our words wisely and structuring our sentences to make the most impact and bring joy to other people's lives.

A Change in Perspective

A couple years ago, I found myself waiting in line at the airport. I have TSA Precheck, which means I use a shorter and faster line than everyone else, but for some reason my TSA Precheck was not showing up on my account that day and I had to wait in the long, "normal" TSA line. Now, this may not seem like a big deal, but when you travel as much as I do for work this seemingly minor inconvenience was a test of patience (that I failed at the time).

Anyway, to say I was upset would be an understatement. First, I started getting upset about taking off my shoes. Then, I started getting upset about taking my laptop out of my bag. (Both of which you don't have to do in the Precheck line.) I was fuming when the guy next to me asked how my day was. I immediately answered with, "It would be a whole lot better if I didn't have to wait in this hot mess." He smiled and responded with, "Well, the airport is always an adventure!"

I was shocked how his positive words gave me a whole new perspective on the situation. I also became aware of how my negative words reflected poorly on me and my attitude.

Do you see the difference a few words can make? What if that gentlemen was an event planner who could hire me and found out that I was a speaker on helping people reach higher than they ever thought possible? Do you think that he'd still want to hire me after that? Probably not.

That's when I decided to watch my words and choose them more carefully. You just never know who's listening. And, you never know how your words are going to affect someone else. Luckily for me, the guy next to me in the airport line was an angel in disguise.

What if he was having a bad day, too, and my words sent him over the edge? Now, I'm not saying our words determine other people's actions. But we should be held accountable for the words we choose. And we should use our words to lift others up, no matter the situation or circumstance.

Listen, when words hit a trigger spot inside our heart, we remember them forever.

Who Has Touched Your Heart?

Let's play another game. This time, I want you to use the space provided on page 64 and draw a picture of someone in your life who has lifted your spirits with their words. This can be someone you look up to, or a stranger who made your day, or someone who said something to change your life for the positive.

Disclaimer: I couldn't draw a nice picture if my life
depended on it. I am not asking you to draw
the next Mona Lisa. A simple stick figure will
do. But if you have the skillset, feel free to
do your best.

Now, why did you draw this person? Did you choose this person because he or she was honest? Did you choose this person because he or she has amazing ethics? Did you choose this person because he or she always builds you up? Why did you choose this person?

_____

_____

_____

No matter the reason you drew this particular person, I am happy someone came to mind. I have done this exercise many times, and most of the time I draw someone different – which is totally okay as long as they mean something to you.

Let me ask you a question: Have you told this person what their words have meant to you? Have you thanked them for their kind, uplifting, or maybe even life-changing words?

If not, I want to present a challenge to you. In the next 24 hours, I challenge you to reach out to them (via email, social media message, handwritten letter, phone call, or tell them in person) and tell them THANK YOU and tell them how their words changed your life.

You can go into depth or keep your demonstration of gratitude short. It's up to you. The point is to reach out and thank the person for saying something that means so much to you.

NOTE: If the person you drew has passed on, you can write a letter and either put it away or burn it. Or, you are welcome to pick someone living and do this exercise again.

We all love hearing praise and we all want others to build us up. In order to receive more praise, we must give more praise.

Whose Heart Have You Touched?

If I was to ask someone else to draw someone special in their life, do you think they would draw you? I hope so.

And if you aren't in anyone's drawing box yet, I promise you that if you lift others up with motivational and encouraging words, you soon will be.

Be the person who lifts people up with your words. Be the person who helps others reach higher.

" A few careless
words might not
seem like much to
you but may stick
with someone else
for a lifetime.
— Ashley Brinton

Chapter 7
Turn Your Goals into Habits

Habits are routines that you don't have to think about anymore. For instance, do you have to be reminded to brush your teeth, or be reminded to get dressed, comb your hair, or eat a meal?

Most of us don't have to be reminded about these tasks anymore because we've created a habit to complete them. In other words, we perform these tasks everyday – automatically – without any thought or attention.

What other habits do you have? Do you scroll through Instagram on your way to your next class? Do you watch your favorite show while you eat lunch? Do you eat the bottom half of the Oreo before the top half? (Am I the only one who does that?!)

Wouldn't it be nice to have all of your goals set up like this – as habits – so you don't have to think about them anymore? I can tell you from experience that turning your goals into habits makes your life much easier.

But how do you turn a goal into a habit? Here are six steps to turn your goals into habits…

Step 1 – Start Simple

Creating new habits requires you to redirect a portion of your time and attention away from something you already do, so you can focus on the new habit(s). That's why it's important to start simple.

Honestly, this step is always the hardest for me to put into practice because I like to dive in and do EVERYTHING at once. But doing everything at once can be overwhelming and draining for most people – me included.

That's why the best solution is to start simple, by beginning with one goal and making that one goal a habit before making any other goals a habit. Then, after you make that one goal a habit, you can move on to the next goal and make it a habit. And so on and so forth until all of your goals are habits. Make sense?

Step 2 – Identify the Time You Need

Like I mentioned in Step 1, creating new habits requires you to redirect a portion of your time and attention away from something you already do and onto the new habit. Sometimes you'll enjoy this process.

And sometimes your new habit will require you to sacrifice one task you enjoy doing but is not helping you reach your goals with another task that you may or may not enjoy but will help you reach your goals.

In either case, you'll want to identify the time required to create your new habit and acknowledge what other activity you'll have to sacrifice or replace. Doing so will help ease any pain involved with the creation of your new habit and set you up for the success you crave.

Step 3 – Insert "Pain" into the Equation

According to psychologists, humans do things for one of two reasons: to gain pleasure or avoid pain. My parents were masters at this game (thank goodness) and knew how to add just enough "pain" into the equation to get me to do something – and make the task a habit.

When I was growing up, I had chores. My chores were to pick up the dog poop, clean my room, fold the laundry, and dust the baseboards every week. In addition, I was to put the dishes in the dishwasher the moment I finished using them. Nothing hard or out of the ordinary, right?

Here's where the pain comes in. If I didn't do a chore on my list, then I had to go outside on Saturday and either pick a bucket of weeds or a bucket of moldy fruit that had fallen from the fruit trees.

Now, you'd think the easy and simple chores would get done, and I could avoid the painful job of picking weeds and fruit. But you'd be wrong.

For the first year or so after getting my chores assigned to me, I never set aside time during the week to actually do my chores. Instead, I goofed off all week and ended up outside doing the worst job ever!

To make the pain even worse, my dad didn't just give me (and my siblings who didn't finish their chores) a normal size bucket. He gave us the biggest bucket in the world!

And… he wouldn't just let us fill the bucket and be done. No, no, no. When we filled the bucket, he would step inside the bucket with one foot and flatten all the weeds, so the weeds were packed down and you could fit more weeds inside the bucket.

There were some Saturdays I spent ALL DAY picking weeds and moldy fruit off the ground! As you can imagine, this job totally sucked.

Now, I don't tell you this so you feel bad for me. I'm grateful to my parents for this lesson because I learned that if you create enough pain in a specific situation, you'll get off your butt and achieve what you really desire.

Personally, I was a slow learner. Like I mentioned earlier, it took me about a year to realize that if I just did my chores, I would not have to go outside and pick weeds and moldy fruit.

I remember very clearly the moment I realized that fact. It was like a lightning bolt struck me. I thought, "Wait a second... if I do my chores, then I can go outside and play with my friends on Saturday. If I do my chores, then I don't have to pick up moldy fruit anymore!"

That, my friend, is when the habit of doing my chores was created. Not only did I start doing my chores on a consistent basis, I started doing my chores every Monday, so I could get them out of the way.

Step 4 – Plan for the Obstacles

Now, even though I "planned" to do my chores on Monday, sometimes obstacles, like school activities, homework, neighborhood events, etc., got in the way.

But that's natural, and we must understand that is going to happen. After all, "stuff" happens, right? So, instead of getting discouraged, it's important for us to have a plan for the obstacles, so we can complete a task and achieve our goals.

In my case, every time an obstacle prevented me from doing my chores on Monday, I would wake up earlier on Tuesday morning and get my chores done. That was my "Plan B." that was a secondary habit I created. Plan A was to get the chores done on Monday, and that habit triggered more often than not. Plan B was a secondary habit that triggered when Plan A went out the window.

Again, if you plan how you will handle the obstacles that come up, you will find yourself accomplishing your goals. If you don't have a plan for the obstacles, you will probably find yourself not completing the task, goal, or habit at all and getting frustrated with yourself.

Step 5 – Work on Your Habit Every Day for 30 Days

When you want to turn a goal into a habit, it's important to work on your habit every day for at least 30 days. That way, you condition your brain to act on the goal and crave the feeling of accomplishing the task.

For example, it's been reported that people who make their beds in the morning have a sense of accomplishment before their day even starts. Hence, the military makes soldiers make their beds first thing in the morning. It's not because the military wants the beds to look nice. It's because they want soldiers to learn the value of their habits and have more confidence in their day.

Does turning a goal into a habit take time? Of course it takes time. Habits take about 30 days to solidify in your brain. But all great goals in life take time, energy, and effort. That's what makes reaching your goals so worthwhile.

So, don't concern yourself with the time it will take you to turn a goal into a habit. Instead, focus on the results you'll achieve when your habits help you create the life you've always dreamed of.

And if you have trouble remembering to act on your goals to create your habits, set a reminder on your phone to complete your tasks. Yes, your phone can be used for more than communicating with friends and watching funny videos. Your phone can be a secret weapon to help you turn your goals into habits and your habits into lifelong accomplishments!

Step 6 – Give Yourself a "Get Out of Jail Free Card"

While setting goals and creating habits are critical to your success and your ability to reach higher, it's also important to not be too hard on yourself. Yes, I believe you should have high expectations and take the necessary actions. But learning to occasionally give yourself some grace will help you stay motivated and enjoy the journey. That's why I suggest giving yourself a "get out of jail free card" every now and then (once a week max).

There you have it. Six steps to help you turn your goals into habits. In the next chapter, I'll show you a simple yet profound way to keep yourself accountable and help you reach your goals (and create habits) faster.

Chapter 8
Tell the World

When I was in college, a professor of mine gave our class an assignment. First, we had to create five S.M.A.R.T. goals. Then, we had to film ourselves talking about our goals and post the video to social media and YouTube. Finally, if we had five or more views on the video, we would get extra credit.

To be totally honest, I didn't like the assignment, but I did it anyway, so I could pass the class. And, to ensure I received all the points I could, I asked my family and friends to watch the video. I ended up with a short video about my five goals with seven views.

My professor told us that having our goals out in the world would help us make our goals come to life. I was a little unsure what he meant by that, but a few months later I was at a family gathering when my YouTube video became the hot topic around the dinner table. I actually hadn't thought twice about my goals since the assignment. but there I was at the dining room table getting asked about my goals and if I needed any help making them come true.

For the first time, I felt like I had cheerleaders on the outside cheering me on in my personal goals. It was crazy, everyone at the table actually cared how I was doing with my goals. That's when I realized what my professor meant...

When we tell the world about our goals, the world holds us accountable to our dreams.

Believe it or not, other people want to see you succeed. But unless you tell them what you're trying to do and how you see success for yourself, it's hard for others to help you. That's one reason why telling the world about your goals is so important.

But that's not all. Another reason telling the world helps you achieve more is because most of us would do anything to avoid the guilt and embarrassment of not achieving what we said out loud to other people.

For example, have you ever told anyone that you were going to do something and then completely forgot to do it? I have. We all have. How did that make you feel? Guilty? Embarrassed? Ashamed?

While these negative emotions don't feel very good to experience, these feelings can be the driving force you need to hold yourself accountable, achieve your goals, and reach higher than you ever thought possible.

So, here's your assignment:

Tell the World About Your Goals

Take your S.M.A.R.T. goals from each success category and…

1. Film yourself talking about your S.M.A.R.T. goals and how you plan to reach them.

2. Post your video on YouTube and other social media platforms.

3. Ask friends and family to watch your video and ask them to keep you accountable.

It's that simple. I promise you that once you tell the world about your goals, the world will help you stay true to yourself and reach higher than ever before.

In the next chapter, I'll show you eight ways to become a better you!

Chapter 9
Become a Better You

When you focus on making yourself better, everything in life gets easier. That's why, in this chapter, I want to share with you eight quick tips on how you can become the best version of yourself.

Tip #1 – Compliment Yourself Every Day

What are you telling yourself when you wake up in the morning? What are you saying to yourself when no one else is around you? Positive self-talk can change your frame of mind and brighten your day. So, start your day by giving yourself a compliment first thing in the morning (and whenever you look in the mirror). Look in the mirror and tell yourself something that you are proud of. Complement yourself on the way you look (new haircut, great outfit)…on the way you communicate with others…on how you make other people feel special…on how you kicked butt on your test this week…on how you made new friends this year…on the

actions you took yesterday and how you completed everything on your to-do list. You get the idea.

Give yourself a compliment every day and change the way
you see yourself. Doing so will help you see the good inside
you and increase your self-confidence. In addition, when you
compliment yourself every day, the positive emotions you
feel toward yourself and life will be contagious and affect
other people in your life.

Try it now. Write some compliments you can give yourself.

_____

_____

_____

Now, go to the mirror and give yourself a few compliments.
How did that make you feel?

_____

_____

_____

Tip #2 – Start Your Day with a Morning Routine

Whether you consider yourself a morning person or a night
owl, you can benefit from waking up every morning and

starting your day with a morning routine. What is a morning routine? A morning routine is a set pattern or process you follow to start your day. Your routine can be as long or as short as you'd like, but I suggest you try to have the first hour of your day stay the same.

Why? Because when you're able to take control of your first hour, you set yourself up for success the rest of the day. And instead of living your life in default mode or on someone else's schedule, you start every morning on purpose – the way you want to start your day!

When I was in college, I had a water aerobics class that started at 6:00AM. Before I started living my life with a morning routine, I found myself waking up at 5:45AM, sleepily putting on my swimsuit, running to class, and barely making it on time. No breakfast. No packing my backpack for the rest of the day. Nothing. Of course, the water woke me up, but my attitude for the rest of the day was rushed and angry.

It wasn't until the next semester that I learned a better way of doing things. You see, the next semester I still had my 6:00AM water aerobics class. But this time, I also had a 7:30AM English class. Meaning, there was no way I would be able to go from my water aerobics class, back home to get ready, and back out the door to make my English class. It wasn't going to happen.

Instead, I had to go from water aerobics straight to English. This meant I had to pack my backpack for the rest of the day *before* I could leave for my water aerobics class. So, rather than waking up at 5:45AM as I had the semester before, I decided to wake up at 5:00AM and get ready for the day. Now, I'd like to tell you that I planned to start my day with a consistent morning routine, but that would be a lie. Even so, something amazing happened...

Water aerobics turned into my favorite class, and my attitude on those days was beyond happy. The time of the class didn't change. The temperature of the water didn't change. I was actually waking up earlier on water aerobics days (and I swear the water was a tinge colder!), but I found myself enjoying the day more and getting more done. That's when I discovered the power of a morning routine.

Everyone's morning routine is slightly different, but to give you a little insight into how you can create your own morning routine, here's how I spend the first hour of my day:

1. Wake up and take the dog to the bathroom

2. Drink a glass of water

3. Stretch – this helps me shake off grogginess and get ready for the day

4. Shower

5. Brush my teeth and get dressed

6. Write in my journal from the day before

7. Read something positive or something that will help me reach my goals

8. Brain Dump – This is a chance for me to write down everything that is on my mind. Sometimes I create a to -do list, other times I just get things out of my head, so I can clear my mind for the day.

9. Daily Goals – After I brain dump, I come up with daily goals – the top three things I MUST get done – to help me move forward on my bigger goals and feel accomplished that day.

10. Eat breakfast!

Now it's your turn. What can you do every morning to set yourself up for success? Use the space below and write out how you would like your morning routine to look:

_____

_____

_____

Tip #3 – Put Yourself in Airplane Mode

Have you ever been on an airplane? If not, one of the first things the flight attendants ask you to do is put your phone in "airplane mode" – which disables all of the Bluetooth, Wi-Fi, cellular, and data connections.

In doing so, you shut the world out for a while. No calls. No texting. No notifications. But that's not a bad thing, because you can now tap into your own thoughts, have the ability to read something, have the opportunity to make the stranger next to you a friend, and/or get work done away from distractions – except, of course, when the attendants bring snacks!

So, why am I telling you about airplane mode? Because in order for you to reach higher than you ever have before, I suggest you set aside at least one day a week to go into airplane mode and shut the world out for a while. Doing so will allow you to concentrate on your thoughts and stay focused on whatever task or goal you are currently working on.

Tip #4 – Make Better Use of Your Time

Have you ever found a $10 bill in your pocket? Feels pretty good, doesn't it? But let me ask you this…have you ever found an extra 10 minutes in your pocket? Of course not! That's because you can't "find" time to do anything. It's impossible. But you can learn to make better use of your time.

And making better use of your time starts with a simple mindset shift. Instead of saying, "I wish I could find the time," tell yourself the truth by saying, "I already have the time, I just need to use my time better."

Tip #5 – Learn from Your Mistakes

It's easy to point fingers and make excuses for why you aren't happy or successful in your personal or professional life. But blaming other people or circumstances won't help you reach higher or get what you want. Instead, it's important to own your mistakes and learn from them.

Listen, we all make mistakes! The goal is to not make the same mistakes over and over again. That's why learning from your mistakes is crucial for your success (and sanity).

So, how do you start learning from your mistakes? First, acknowledge the fact that you will make mistakes. Lots of them! Then, when you make your next mistake, accept all the blame and ask yourself: what can I learn from this? Finally, forgive yourself and move forward.

Yes, this is easier said than done. And, yes, this may take some time to practice. But once you start learning from your mistakes and you learn to forgive yourself, you will be further along your journey to success, and you will be happier than ever before.

Tip #6 – Put a Period on It

Have you ever been in a situation where someone is telling you every little detail about his or her day or about his or her life? It's true, some of us can get a little over-excited and tell people more than we probably should (and more than they'd prefer to know).

If you're one of those people (and I'll admit I'm one), it's important to realize that sometimes less is more and we need to "put a period on it."

Doing so will give you an opportunity to listen more, learn more, and experience more.

Tip #7 – Avoid the Rotten Apple

Did you know that one moldy apple can cause the entire bunch of apples to go bad and spoil? This happens because the mold quickly spreads and looks for a new food source. The same concept applies to humans. When one person is having a bad day, everyone around that person seems to have a bad day too.

Now, I'm not saying that you can avoid bad days or that the people around you can skip over a bad day. We all have bad days. However, it's crucial to your well-being that you try to avoid people who are ALWAYS having a bad day. Those people are rotten apples. And if you're not careful, their attitude will cause you to "spoil."

Tip #8 – Find a Hobby

Hobbies help you clear your mind. Some people sew or knit. Some people play sports or video games. Some people paint or color (yes, adults can color too!). Personally, I love board games. Board games relax me and bring back all kinds of happiness.

What is your hobby? What helps you clear your mind?

_____

_____

_____

So, there you have it. Eight tips to help you become the best version of yourself. In the next chapter, we'll explore how you can create your own reality.

Chapter 10
You Create Your Own Reality

The first step to creating your own reality is understanding that you are 100% responsible for your life and the choices you make.

When I was in grade school, my fifth-grade teacher had us repeat the classroom creed after the school announcements and the Pledge of Allegiance. Here is the creed:

I AM RESPONSIBLE FOR MY DAY

I am responsible for how I feel and for what I do.

Nobody can make me feel anything.

If I have a rotten day, I am the only one who allowed
it to be that way.

If I have a great day, I am the one who deserves credit
for being positive.

It is not the responsibility of other people to change so
that I can feel better.

I AM THE ONE WHO IS RESPONSIBLE FOR MY LIFE!!

I don't just remember the classroom creed to this day because
I recited it every day that year (though I'm sure that helps). I
believe that I still remember the classroom creed because of
the impact it had on my life.

You see, we all have choices. Being responsible doesn't mean
we have to like our choices. Being responsible means that we
are in control and we are in charge of the choices we make.

For example, if someone insults you, you have a choice. You
can *choose* to take what he or she said to heart and let their
mean-spirited words tear you down. Or, you can *choose* to
ignore his or her comments and let their words go in one ear
and out the other – without ever making you doubt yourself.
You have that choice. His or her words can't make you feel
one way or another. You are responsible for how you choose
to feel – no matter what happens to you.

Of course, the choices you make aren't limited to dealing
with other people. You have the ability to make choices and
be responsible in all areas of your life.

Seeing the Good in Any Situation

The second step to creating your own reality is seeing the
good in any situation. Listen, sometimes stuff happens that

makes us feel like life sucks. But if you can learn (and train yourself) to see the good in any situation, you'll realize that life is amazing and awesome.

My four-year-old niece told me she wanted to be a Disney Princess. I told her in order to do that she would have to go to Princess school, study calligraphy, grow to the perfect height requirement, and, of course, never stop smiling!

She shrugged and said, "that's just four things!"

My niece didn't see the obstacles in her way. She only saw the good in what I was saying – there are only four things she has to do to become a Disney Princess.

I love my niece and her attitude about life! Nothing is going to stop her. And if you understand this concept, nothing is going to stop you in your life!

So, to help you learn to see the good in any situation, let's play another game. This time I want you to look at the table on page 94.

On the left side, we have situations where we may feel that LIFE SUCKS. On the right side, we have the choice to see how LIFE IS AWESOME in spite of what's happening in the other column. You'll see that I gave you a few examples.

Follow my lead and use the left column to write down a list of things that totally suck in your life right now. Then, use the right column to flip everything around and see the good in the situation.

Life Sucks	Life Is Awesome
I sit alone at lunch.	I sit alone at lunch… which is awesome because I get to eat all my own tater tots.
I didn't make the lead in the school play.	I didn't make the lead in the school play… which is awesome because I get to better myself by reading this book.

As you can see, my right column has fun, silly answers. Feel free to make light of the situation and have fun with this game. Using humor can lighten your mood and make you realize how frivolous, silly, or superficial an event or situation truly is.

The bottom line is this: you create your own reality through the choices you make and how you see the world around you.

"

Instead of complaining that the rose bush is full of thorns, be happy the thorn bush has roses.

— Proverb

"

Chapter 11
Taste Your Dreams

Here's the scenario: in front of you are five containers, each holding a meal that I've cooked for you. The only problem is the containers are covered, and you have no idea what I've prepared for you or if you'll like the meal. Now, let me ask you this: if I told you that you could only eat one meal the rest of your life, which option would you choose?

Option 1: You can choose one meal at random and eat that meal the rest of your life.

Option 2: You can taste test each meal and then decide which meal you'll eat for the rest of your life.

Which option would you choose? Most people would choose Option 2, because the chance of choosing a meal at random and getting a meal that you enjoy enough to eat every day is not worth the risk.

The same can be said about your dream career.

Yes, I know that you may really want to be a fireman, a doctor, a school teacher, a lawyer, an engineer, etc. But unless you taste your dreams first, you may choose a career that leaves a bad taste in your mouth, or even makes you sick.

My husband had that experience. You see, my husband always dreamed of working in sports. He spent over $30,000 earning his Bachelor of Arts in Communications with an emphasis in Sports Media. Then, he landed a job at the local news station and started to produce the sports segment. He accomplished his dream, working in sports!

However, it didn't feel amazing and awesome like he always dreamed it would be. In fact, he started to really hate his job, feeling upset and frustrated. Eventually, he became so sick of his job that he had to switch careers to keep his sanity.

Don't you think it would have been nice if we would have known that before he went down the path he did – wasting tens of thousands of dollars and putting unnecessary stress on himself (and the people around him)? Not to mention all the time it took.

I don't want the same to happen to you. So, to avoid the pain of randomly choosing a career path that you hate, here are three ways to "taste" your dream career before making any major decisions:

1. Job Shadow – If you haven't already chosen a career path, connect with people who have your potential dream career and job shadow them for a day, or as

long as you can. Shadowing someone is the quickest way to determine if the path you want to take is the right path for you.

2. Become an Intern – If you have already chosen a career path, intern with a company in your chosen field as soon as possible. Living your dream and/or seeing other people living your dream day in and day out as an intern will give you insight into what your life will look like. If you're still excited after your internship, then you're one of the lucky ones who randomly chose a meal that you get to enjoy for the rest of your life. However, if you hated every second of your internship, then count your blessings, because there is still time to change your mind.

3. Try Different Jobs – If you have no idea what career path is right for you, then take this opportunity to try every job you can think of before deciding on a career. The job that lights a fire inside you is the job that will make you happy for the rest of your life.

Chapter 12
Be Brave

According to a scientific experiment, fleas are one of the best jumpers of all known animals and can jump over 200 times their body height. However, when fleas are placed in a jar with a lid on top, the fleas will only jump as high as the lid – without smacking into the lid. In addition – and this is fascinating – when you take the lid off the jar, the fleas won't jump out, because they've been conditioned to only jump as high as the lid.

So, why are we talking about fleas? Because most humans are no different than fleas in a jar. No, we cannot fit into a jar or jump as high as a flea (though that would be really awesome). But sometimes, when we move towards our dreams, we let our self-imposed lid (challenges, dis-abilities, etc.), or someone else's lid (opinions, negative viewpoints, etc.), prevent us from reaching our true potential. Instead, we need to learn how to break through the lid, so we can reach higher and achieve what we were destined to achieve.

But how? How can we break through the lids that are holding us back from reaching higher? First, we must be brave and…

Face Your Challenges Head On

Being brave doesn't mean that we don't have struggles or dis
-abilities or challenges. Being brave means that we see our
struggles, dis-abilities, and challenges and face them head on
– no matter how scary they may seem.

Is being brave easy? No way! Being brave is hard. I know this
feeling intimately. You see, when I was in eighth grade, we
had a career festival at our school. The first part of the day
involved each student walking around and learning the basics of their chosen career (i.e. what we wanted to be when
we grew up): how to pay taxes, how many paid holidays we
would have, how much money we could make, what benefits
we may receive, etc. The second part of the day involved an
assembly with a career counselor, who talked about the future and our dream careers.

He asked for volunteers to share what they wanted to be
when they grew up. Of course, I raised my hand. I knew I
wanted to be a keynote speaker! But to my surprise, when I
told the career counselor that, "I want to be a keynote speaker, "he asked me a series of arrogant questions.

"Do you personally know any keynote speakers?"

"No," I replied.

He snobbishly came back with, "Has anybody in your family ever given a paid speech on stage?"

"No," I replied – still proud and excited about my decision.

He then tossed my dream aside and said "You can't be a keynote speaker, that's not a realistic career. Who else wants to share their dream career?"

This career counselor didn't ask me for a "realistic" career. He asked me what I wanted to be. I told him. But instead of encouraging me, he decided to place a lid on me and move onto the next person.

I was devastated. Angry. Hurt. I was crying on the inside and everyone in the room (the entire eighth grade class) could tell how embarrassed I was.

What did I do? Admittedly, his comments were damaging to me for quite some time. But I wasn't about to allow someone to put a lid on me and squash my dreams. I wanted to be a keynote speaker – no matter what anyone else said. So, I kept my dream in my heart and I jumped so high and so hard that I broke through that lid.

Today, I am a full-time keynote speaker, enjoying my dream career and writing this book to share my failures, successes, and stories with you in the hopes that my experiences help you reach higher and achieve your dreams – no matter what your dreams are!

Now, I don't tell you any of this to boost my ego. I'm telling you this because how often do we allow others to affect our direction, our attitude, our altitude, or our ability? How often do we allow others to tell us how high we can reach? Far too often, in my opinion.

To achieve our dreams and desires, we must stop looking to the left and right to see what others are doing, and we must stop basing our actions on someone else's thoughts, opinions, and criticisms. To reach higher and achieve our dreams, we must go out in the world and be brave!

Free Yourself from Your Jar

If you're ready to free yourself from your jar and break through your lids, there are two additional steps you must take beyond being brave. First, you must identify the lid(s) holding you captive. Then, you must take the necessary steps to unscrew or break through your lid(s).

Before I went off on my own and became a full-time keynote speaker, I worked a full-time job at a company that allowed me to speak to their audiences. I honestly thought I would work there for the rest of my life because I was living my dream as a speaker, and I loved the idea of what my job could be. But after asking several times if I could be put on other projects and getting some type of "lid on my jar" answer, I realized that my current full-time job wasn't my dream career. Yes, I loved some parts of my job. But I knew a lid was on… and it was on tight!

Are you in a similar situation? Do you have a lid on your jar? Here are some questions to help identify if you have a lid on your jar:

- Are you excited about waking up in the morning?

- Even though you keep checking things off your to-do list, do you feel unfulfilled?

- Do people tell you that you can't or that you're not good enough?

- Are you sick of hearing yourself complain?

- Do you have so much time in your day that you find yourself feeling bored and available to do anything anyone asks?

- Do you feel comfortable where you are - even though you know you would be happier if you made a change in your life?

Your answers to the above questions will help you identify if you have any lids on your jar. If you discover a lid or two, then I encourage you to break through your lid(s) by being brave and taking the next, logical step.

What's the next step? I don't know. You'll have to figure that out for yourself, based on where you are and the lid(s) you have holding you captive. For me, I broke through my lid (my limiting job) by coming up with a plan to start my own speaking business and taking the steps to make it happen. I don't know your next steps, but I believe in you and I know you can figure this out.

If you feel like you're in a jar with lids holding you in, then take a moment now and answer this question: What action do I need to take to free myself from this lid and my jar?

_____

_____

_____

"

If you can't fly,
then run. If you
can't run, then
walk. If you can't
walk, then crawl.
But whatever you
do, you have to
keep moving
forward.

— Martin Luther King

Chapter 13
Wisdom Comes
from Failure

When a baby is learning how to walk, he or she falls over and over and over again. But does the baby stop trying just because he or she "failed"? No! Every baby learning to walk, who has the ability to walk, gets up off his or her butt and tries again. And again. And again. Until one day, he or she can walk!

Listen, failing is a part of life. And failure is part of the process to your success. Warren Buffett, one of the richest, most successful people on our planet, has said numerous times that he would not invest in any business where the owner hasn't failed at least twice.

Failing and failure are normal and necessary. So, be grateful for the time you burned your hand on the stove top when you were a kid. Be grateful for the time when you locked yourself out of the house in the winter. Be grateful for the time you messed up a test. You have failed in your life. You will fail again. But realize that all of your failures have brought you wisdom. The wisdom to keep your hands away from hot stove tops. The wisdom to always bring your keys with you wherever you go. The wisdom to study harder next time you have a test. The wisdom to keep trying. The wisdom to never give up. And much, much more!

What Have You Learned?

In the table on page 112, I want you to write down a list of all your "failures" over the past few months. Maybe you failed a test (or did worse than you thought you would). Maybe you said something you didn't mean to a friend. Maybe you had an embarrassing situation at home or at school. Whatever you think is a "failure," write it down on page 112.

Good job. Now, I want you to write down any valuable lessons (wisdom) you learned from each of your failures. For example, if you failed a test, did you (or will you) study harder for the next test? If you said something to a friend that you didn't mean to, did you engage them in a conversation and apologize? What did you learn from your mistakes, failures and "oops"?

Great job! Now, let me ask you a question: if you had to choose one of the following options, which one would you choose?

1.   Keep both your failures and your wisdoms

2.   Throw away your failures and keep your wisdoms

"

It is impossible to live without failing at something, unless you live so cautiously that you might as well not have lived at all, in which case you have failed by default.

— J.K. Rowling

"

Failure	Wisdom

3. Throw away your wisdoms and keep your failures

4. Throw away both your failures and your wisdoms

While there's no "right" answer, I sincerely hope you chose number one because wisdom comes from failure. In other words, you can't gain wisdom without failing first. Failure is a learning opportunity. Failure teaches us things we don't already know, or reminds us of what we should know. Wisdom and failure go hand in hand. You can't have one without the other.

Better an Oops Than a What If

There is one emotion that can stop us in our tracks and prevent us from gaining the wisdom failure brings our way – fear. Fear of failure stops us from even trying. And when we don't try, we have regret. At least that's what I've experienced.

I have found that when I let the fear of failing stop me from acting, I have regret, I feel sad, and I am disappointed in myself. However, I've also discovered that when I push past my fear and I choose to act in spite of fear, I feel better about myself, because I tried!

I don't know about you, but I'd rather try something and have to say, "Oops" than walk away without trying and think to myself, "I wonder what would or could have happened if I would have tried that."

The oops in life don't scare me. The what ifs do.

So, do me a favor and jot down why you fear failure in the octagon on page 114.

Why Do You Fear Failure?
(Write your answers in the octagon below.)

Now, lay this book down flat and PUNCH your fear right in the face. Yes, you read that correctly. I want you to lay this book down, take your fist, and punch, smack, and hit this page.

Don't let the fear of failure stop you from reaching higher and achieving your dreams. Be brave and punch your fear in the face. Your fear doesn't own you or control you. You control how you feel. You control your fear.

Chapter 14
Normal Is an Illusion

Like I mentioned earlier, when I was younger, I was diagnosed with a reading dis-ability. What I didn't tell you was that my left eye read straight (which is how your eye is supposed to read) and my right eye read in circles. As you can imagine, because my eyes weren't working together, reading was a difficult task that required more time and concentrated effort on my part. So, in fourth grade, I started eye therapy.

Eye therapy took up most of my time after school. Some days I would go to the eye doctor and either take computer tests or have private reading sessions, where I would have to catch a ball in one hand while reading what was on the wall with only my right eye (my left eye was covered). Other days I had an in-house eye tutor, who would make me jump on a trampoline while reading so my eyes would learn how to focus better. And when I wasn't doing eye therapy at the doctors or at home, I was at my reading tutor's house; reading books and writing book reports together.

So, in all reality, after school was no "play time with friends" for me. After school involved more school work and more learning, so I could condition my eyes to read better.

Was it easy? Of course not. I remember staring out the window and wishing I could go outside and play with my friends. For a 10-year-old kid, it was hard to understand why I was different. Why I had to sit inside learning when everyone else was outside having a good time. Why I couldn't just be "normal."

Maybe you feel the same way. Maybe you, too, used to wonder why you were different. Maybe you still do. Asking yourself, "Why me?" is a dangerous practice. After all, asking "Why me?" never conjures up a good answer. Instead of your brain coming up with good reasons, your brain comes up with the worst answers possible.

[You] I have a reading dis-ability…why me?

[Your brain] Because you're stupid. Because no one likes you. Because… because… because…

When you ask yourself, "Why me?" does your brain give you worthless answers, too? Questioning why I have a reading dis-ability didn't help me improve my reading. It just made me feel worse.

That's when I came to the hard realization that it didn't matter why I had a reading dis-ability. The fact is I did have a reading dis-ability, and nothing was going to change that.

The only thing I could do was move forward and deal the hand I was dealt.

Now, I can't tell you that this was a quick process. It took me a while to understand that there was no such thing as normal - that normal is an illusion. Being different and unique is a part of life. Being different and unique is what makes me, me and you, you. Being different and unique *is* normal.

Stop asking yourself, "Why me?" Stop being ashamed of who you are. And stop feeling embarrassed because of your challenge, struggle, or dis-ability.

Just be you...and let the rest of the world figure out why you're awesome. Because you are. And because they will.

"

Whatever makes
you weird, is
probably your
greatest asset.

— Joss Whedon

"

Chapter 15
Apples and Oranges

W hen I was in high school, my neighbor gave me the following story on a small piece of paper. Even though its edges are worn and ripped, I've kept this story with me over the years and I have it taped to my wall in my office.

Ever since I was a little girl, I didn't want to be me.
I wanted to be like Natalie Daly, and she didn't even like
me. I walked like she walked, talked like she talked. Which
was why I soon saw that she changed. She began to hang
with Heidi Smith, she walked like Heidi talked like Heidi.
So, I began to talk and walk like Natalie Daly trying to
walk and talk like Heidi Smith. Then it dawned on me, that
Heidi Smith walked and talked like Zoe Jones and Zoe
walked and talked like Joanne Rain. So here I am walking
and talking like Natalie Daly, imitation of Heidi Smith,
version of Zoe Jones trying to walk and talk like Joanne
Rain. And who do you think Joanne is always walking and
talking like? Of all people, Savanah William, that little
pest who walks and talks just like me.

Good or bad, like Savanah, we all compare ourselves to other people. I used to compare myself to other girls in school, other employees at work, and other motivational speakers. I'd be lying to you if I told you I've stopped comparing myself to other people completely. It does happen on occasion.

But I have to remind myself about this story and how everyone wanted to be like someone else. Not because we can't improve and be better when we see other people who inspire us. But because comparing yourself to other people is like comparing an apple to an orange.

Yes, they are both fruits, but they are completely different. They look different. They smell different. They taste different. Therefore, comparing an apple to an orange is a waste of time.

You and I are like apples and oranges. We're both people. But we look different. We act different. And we are different. So, like comparing apples and oranges is a waste of time, so is comparing ourselves to each other.

Perhaps our time would be better spent enjoying each other and our differences – just like we enjoy apples and oranges, bananas and grapes, and all the fruits we have at our fingertips.

"

If we all threw our
problems in a pile
and saw everyone
else's we'd grab
ours back.

— Regina Brett

Chapter 16
You Can Only Reach So High By Yourself

My goal throughout this book has been to show you that no matter where you are now or what you have to go through, you can reach higher and you can go beyond your personal limitations, struggles, and challenges to live an awesome life.

However, before we wrap up together, there is an important piece of advice I want to leave you with. That crucial piece of advice is this: You can only reach so high by yourself. But with the help of other people, you can reach even higher!

I know this from experience. You see, when I was in seventh grade, I didn't believe in myself. But a teacher of mine saw my potential and bribed me with a candy bar to attend an FCCLA meeting. Since I love candy, I took the bait and began attending meetings on a regular basis. Then, after a few months of meetings, I found myself attending an FCCLA conference with kids from all over the state.

As my confidence grew, I started networking and making new friends in the organization. And after a year, because of my new relationships, I was nominated to represent my school at the state level. From there I was able to network, build relationships, and communicate with college professors, state government representatives, and so many other amazing people.

In the following two years, those relationships turned into amazing references and allowed me to move up the ladder once again and represent not only my school, but also my state, on a national level, and eventually become an intern in the same organization.

Finally, after four years of networking and building relationships inside that organization, I was handed the contact information for a key decision maker, along with a recommendation letter, which helped me land a job as a coach and speaker.

Could I have done all this without the bonds, relationships, and alliances I had forged since seventh grade? Maybe…but it's highly unlikely. My relationships were the key to my success. They always have been, and they always will be. The same is true in your life. You can reach higher all by yourself. But how high you can reach by yourself pales in comparison to how high you can reach with the help of other people.

So, how do you reach higher with the help of other people? By learning how to…

Network and Build Quality Relationships

There's no secret to networking and building relationships. You don't have to say anything special. You don't have to learn any intricate handshakes. You just have to learn three simple strategies.

First, you have to learn to open your mouth and say "hello!" Say hi to your teachers. Say hi to the rest of the school staff. Say hi to your friends' parents. Say hi to your parents' friends. Say hi to your neighbors. Say hi to everyone and open up as many lines of communication as possible. You never know who can help you reach your dreams.

Second, even though you want to open up as many lines of communication as possible, it's important to understand that high-quality relationships take time and effort. Therefore, please realize that a few high-quality relationships are better than dozens of low-quality connections. That's not to say you shouldn't be friendly or be supportive of everyone you meet. You should, because it's the right thing to do and you never know where your kindness will take you. But since you only have so much time, it's imperative to choose your deep relationships carefully and make them as strong as you can.

Last, you have to realize that building a relationship is not about getting what you want. Building a relationship is about being selfless, making other people feel good about themselves, and helping other people get what they want. When you make others feel better, or help them get what they want, they'll be more inclined to help you in any way they can.

Think about your friends. You would do anything for your true friends, and your true friends would do anything for you. The same is true in all areas of your life and relationships.

All successful people leverage their relationships to reach higher. So, learn these three invaluable strategies and reach higher than ever before!

Your Next Steps

Congratulations, I'm so proud of you for making it all the way through this book! Seriously, most people never read a book cover to cover, myself included, so this is a big deal. You should be proud of yourself! I am.

Now, you may be asking, "Ashley, you don't read every book cover to cover?" While I don't like to admit this, I unfortunately don't finish every book all the way through. Is it because I lose interest? No. Is it because I don't have time? No. In all honesty, I don't finish most books because I don't want them to end. I know that may sound silly, but it's the truth.

So, as I was writing "the end" to this book, I realized something. It's not the end. It's just the beginning. And it's time for you to continue your journey and write your own epic story, complete with a fairy-tale ending.

Listen, you now have the ideas, tactics, strategies, and perspective you need to overcome the struggles, challenges, and obstacles in your life. However, if you're going to reach higher and have the awesome, excellent, extraordinary life you desire and deserve, you must implement what you learned.

But you don't have to do this alone (remember from Chapter 16, you can reach higher with other people's help)! So, to help you on your journey, I want to gift you my *Reach Higher Than You Ever Thought Possible* coaching program absolutely free for reading this book.

I'd love the honor to help you go beyond your personal limitations, struggles, and challenges to live an awesome life and achieve your ultimate potential. You can find details at AshleySpeaks.com/reachhigherprogram and read how the program will help you go beyond this book and help you reach higher in every aspect of your life.

Are you ready to continue this journey with me? Meet me at AshleySpeaks.com/reachhigherprogram and I'll see you there!

Ashley

It's now time to write your story...

_____

_____

_____

_____

_____

_____

_____

_____

_____

_____

_____

_____

_____

_____

_____

_____

_____

_____

_____

The End...

About the Author

At age 15, Ashley Brinton was advised to drop out of high school and never go to college by educational professionals (i.e. teachers). But Ashley was determined. She not only finished high school, she also received a "Woman of the Year in Family Life Studies" award and she earned her bachelor's degree from Utah State University. Ashley is living and walking proof that even though you have struggles, challenges, or a "dis-ability," you can reach higher and achieve your dreams.

From one-on-one consultations to high profile conferences, Ashley travels full-time throughout the country, spreading this empowering, inspiring, and encouraging message to audiences of all ages and backgrounds: "Although life isn't always easy, life can always be fun, and you can always reach higher!"

When Ashley isn't on stage, you can find her traveling the world with her husband, sampling food at Costco, playing board games, or relaxing with the world's cutest goldendoodle, Wiggles.

Are You Looking for a Speaker for Your Next Event?

Your Audience Will Thank You for Choosing Ashley Brinton!

Are you looking for a fun, inspiring speaker who will keep your audience entertained and engaged?

Are you looking for a young female voice who knows how to thoroughly educate your audience, have them sitting on the edge of their seats, and raving about your event afterwards?

Are you looking for a professional who is easy and fun to work with?

If you answered "YES" to any of these questions, then Ashley Brinton is the speaker you've been looking for!

Ashley offers the takeaway tips that audiences need and want and the "wow" factor and professionalism that meeting planners value.

Five Reasons Meeting Planners, Audiences, and Everyone in Between Loves Having Ashley Brinton at Their Event:

1. **Experienced:** By the age of 22, Ashley Brinton had already professionally presented to over 120 audiences and to over 10,000 students and educators.

2. **Relatable:** Ashley's stories connect. Her lessons inspire. And best of all, Ashley's advice sticks. Ashley understands that students today need to be reached in new and innovative ways. For her, it's not about talking at the audience, it's about connecting with the audience where they are.

3. **Fun:** Ashley Brinton is beyond entertaining and her energy fills the room. Your audience is guaranteed to leave more excited than they entered.

4. **Real and Authentic:** You'll hear the good, the bad, and even the ugly that Ashley has experienced on her own journey to reaching higher as she takes your audience on an epic, inspirational rollercoaster of emotions. Your audience will leave feeling motivated, inspired, and confident that they, too, can reach higher – no matter what life throws their way!

5. **A Powerful Coach:** Ashley uses tried and true coaching techniques to inspire your audience to take immediate action, so they can get fast results.

In addition to wowing your audience and making your life easier, Ashley tailors every speech to your goals and your audience's needs. No two speeches are exactly the same. And every speech is guaranteed to be nothing short of awesome!

Hire Ashley Brinton today by contacting her at:
ashley@ashleyspeaks.com
or call 801-623-8331.

Made in the USA
Middletown, DE
30 December 2021

57291196R00082